THE MEANINGS OF MODERN ART

by JOHN RUSSELL

Art Critic, *The New York Times*

VOLUME **6**

AN ALTERNATIVE ART

LOUIS P. GIORGI

THE MUSEUM OF MODERN ART, NEW YORK

I. Henri Matisse
Bathers by a River, 1916–17
The Art Institute of Chicago

The old order fell apart in Europe in August, 1914; and art fell apart with it.

It didn't show all at once. Some people went on making art; some other people went on looking at it. Museums stayed open, exhibitions were held, magazines came out on time. But something had gone down forever: the unity, the stability, the perfected internationalism of the European art scene before 1914. How could it be otherwise, when Braque, Derain, Léger and Apollinaire were in the army on one side and Kirchner, Marc, Macke and Ernst were in the army on the other? What continuity of contact could there be when Mikhail Larionov was wounded in East Prussia while serving with the Russian Army and the heavy-shouldered, self-confident Max Beckmann was broken in mind by his experiences as a German hospital orderly?

One or two people held out. Matisse had so prodigious a power of concentration, and was so armored against outside interference, that he was able to go on producing masterpieces—few, but telling—throughout World War I. "A man who is not at the front feels good for nothing," he wrote in 1916; but a Matisse like the *Bathers by a River* of 1916–17 (pl. I) is an emblem of sublime determination, rather than of privileged inactivity.

There was also one major painter who was actually changed for the better by the war. Fernand Léger found in his service with the French artillery a degree of social and artistic fulfillment which had never come his way before. He loved the look of the guns and their immaculate functioning. He loved his comrades-in-arms for their offhand courage and their frank and incisive manner of speech. For the first time he felt himself a completely integrated member of society. "It was in wartime," he said later, "that I really got my feet on the ground." His paintings in 1913–14 had been concerned mainly with contrasts of abstract form; but life in the trenches soon put an end to that, and in paintings like *The Card Players* (fig. 1) he tried to bring out the lessons of wartime—the oneness of man and machine, the total democracy of the contacts between one enlisted man and another, and the satisfactions of a life lived for one thing and one only.

But in general the effects of World War I were wholly negative. People got out of it, if they got out at all, as damaged human beings—Braque was trepanned in 1915 after being temporarily blinded, Léger was badly gassed in 1917, Macke was killed in 1914, Marc was killed in 1916. Kirchner went into a long depression. ("Before the war so healthy," Kirchner wrote in the year before his suicide, "and since then nothing but sickness.")

World War I was no time, therefore, for the traditional "career in art." Between 1914 and 1918 it was indecent even to think of the long haul from canvas to canvas, exhibition to exhibition, patron to patron, book to eulogious book. Such things were part of a social structure that had been called in question by the extent, and by the horror, of its breakdown. Who would want to show their work in an official exhibition when that same officialdom had prompted the iniquities so vividly described not long after by Winston Churchill in his *World Crisis*: "No truce or parley mitigated the strife of the armies. The wounded died between the lines; the dead mouldered into the soil. Poison gas in many forms stifled or seared the soldiers. Liquid fire was projected upon their bodies. Men fell from the air in flames, or were smothered, often slowly, in the dark recesses of the sea."

The times called for an alternative art—something that would allow the creative instinct to come through at full strength and yet have none of the social or financial connotations of "fine art." Such an art would be a matter of ideas cut to the bone; it would travel light; it might have only a short life and a distribution among half a dozen people. It must be ready for an irreversible break with the past, and it must set no store by location. The artist could not depend on a certain light, a certain rhythm of life, a certain circumambient culture; himself and one suitcase would have to be enough.

Such an art did come about, from 1915 onward. It came about in New York, initially, and it came about later in Zürich, in Cologne, in Hanover, in Berlin and, eventually, in Paris. It was an odd, extreme and sometimes desperate art; but then those were odd, extreme and desperate times. It was not at all unified; its attitudes ranged from a whole-hearted political commitment to a dandified rejection of the outer world *in toto*. There were people who risked lynching for their beliefs, and there were others who thought, with Picabia, that they should change their ideas as often as they changed their shirts. The art in question produced, in Marcel Duchamp's *Large Glass* (pl. VII), what has rightly been called "the most elaborately fabricated art object of this century"; it also produced at least one periodical of which no copy survives and art objects which the observer was invited to destroy. Tempers can still run hot when this alternative art is under discussion; but if any one thing about it is beyond dispute it is the fact that for a year or two, from 1915 onward, its headquarters was in New York.

NEW YORK: HEADQUARTERS OF THE NEW

Three things made this possible: the presence in New York of Marcel Duchamp and, intermittently, of Francis Picabia, the emergence of a new kind of American artist (Man Ray, above all), and the enthusiasm of a small group of new-style American col-

1. (left) Fernand Léger
The Card Players, 1917
Rijksmuseum Kröller-Müller, Otterlo,
Holland

2. (below) Patrick Henry Bruce
Composition II, c. 1916–17
Yale University Art Gallery,
New Haven, Conn.

Patrick Henry Bruce was a student of
Matisse in Paris before 1914, and a
friend of Robert Delaunay. As much as
any American of his generation, he
understood what had happened to
painting, and more especially to color,
in the 20th century. With his intelli-
gence, his carefully nurtured gifts, and
his close personal contacts in Paris, he
could have been one of the leaders of
a new American art; but he preferred
to remain in Paris, where he pursued an
increasingly isolated course. In 1932
he gave up painting and destroyed all
but a few of his canvases; in 1937 he
committed suicide.

lectors. (There was also, of course, the fact that until April, 1917,
the United States remained neutral in World War I.) Collecting
modern art in North America was pioneered at just this time by
John Quinn, the beaky, pertinacious lawyer who had been one
of the prime movers of the Armory Show; by Walter Arensberg,
eventually to have a wing of his own at the Philadelphia Museum; by Arthur Jerome Eddy, one of the great benefactors of
The Art Institute of Chicago; by the bizarre and redoubtable Dr.
Alfred Barnes, founder of the Barnes Collection in Merion, Pa.;
and by Miss Lillie P. Bliss, one of the founders of The Museum
of Modern Art in New York. Add to these Miss Katherine Dreier,
who, with Marcel Duchamp's help and support, formed the
avant-garde collection which is now at Yale, and it becomes clear
that New York from 1915 was exceptionally alert to the new.

The Armory Show traditionally gets the credit for this, and it
is perfectly true that in 1913 it assembled in record time a pano-
rama that on the European side ran from Ingres and Delacroix to
Kandinsky's *Improvisation No. 27* and Brancusi's *The Kiss*. It up-
dated enthusiasms, all around. The Metropolitan Museum of Art

bought its first Cézanne from the Armory Show, for instance, and there was not an American artist of any quality who did not find it in one way or another a tremendous experience. But it should also be said that the bulk of the Armory Show represented a solid, safe taste. If the "new" was naturalized in New York by 1915, Alfred Stieglitz deserves much of the credit. An artist in his own right—with the camera—he had, since 1905, been running a little gallery at the top of a brownstone house at 291 Fifth Avenue. By 1913 regular visitors would have seen sizable shows by Rodin, Toulouse-Lautrec, Matisse (twice) and Picasso. Stieglitz had a nose for the new in American art, too, and he sponsored the debuts of John Marin, Max Weber, Arthur Dove and Georgia O'Keeffe (whom he married). "I am trying," he once said, "to establish an America in which I can breathe as a free man." He believed that America would not always be one of the outer provinces of art: a place from which moneyed people journeyed to France to buy Degas and Renoir. Out of America, something great would come. Stieglitz would have agreed in that context with Ezra Pound, who wrote to a friend in August, 1912, that the American awakening, when it finally came, would "make the Italian Renaissance look like a tempest in a teapot."

Meanwhile the great American public was quite correct in sensing at the Armory Show that Duchamp and Picabia were modern in a sense that Matisse and Picasso and Braque were not. It was not their ambition to become part of the continuum of serious art which in Europe had stretched, unbroken, for eight centuries. In fact they thought that that continuum might just as well come to an end. Matisse and Braque were content to work 12 or 14 hours a day in the hope of ending up in the Louvre; but Duchamp had come to believe by 1915 that the role of the artist was to do things perfectly and do them once only. As for Picabia, he had been in New York at the time of the Armory Show; and he had very much made himself felt, with his swarthy good looks, his flamboyant manner, and his readiness to be distracted from the studio by a fast car, a pretty woman or a first-rate bottle of wine. He was rich—his grandfather had pioneered the construction of a railroad from Madrid to Corunna—and he openly ridi-

3. Man Ray
A.D. MCMXIV, 1914
Philadelphia Museum of Art

Man Ray was not the only artist to be haunted in 1914 by the notion of an army on the move; but there is something particularly vivid about the faceless and monolithic horde which here obeys the order to march.

4. (*right*) Max Weber
Chinese Restaurant, 1915
Whitney Museum of American Art, New York

Weber, an American born in Russia, had studied painting in Paris, where he became engrossed with Cubism. But he also prized very highly the brilliant and unequivocal coloring of American Indian dolls, quilts and blankets; and when he took, as here, a subject from everyday life in Manhattan he gave it a crisp, all-over sparkle which derived as much from American sources as from the graver, more slow-moving procedures of Cubism.

II. Man Ray
The Rope Dancer Accompanies Herself with Her Shadows, 1916
The Museum of Modern Art, New York

Man Ray's *The Rope Dancer* could be called the last in the canon of circus paintings which began with Degas, Seurat and Toulouse-Lautrec. What the painter did was to chart the dancer's progress along the rope in terms of the different shadows which she cast from her lofty perch. By rendering the shadows in terms of flat panels of pure color Man Ray was able to divide up the canvas in a way which can be read either as abstract painting of an incisive and astringent sort or as a veracious portrait of the dancer's unsteady progress.

III. Stanton MacDonald-Wright
*Abstraction on Spectrum
(Organization 5),* 1914
Des Moines Art Center,
Des Moines, Iowa

Among the young American painters
who abounded in Paris before 1914,
Stanton MacDonald-Wright was out-
standing for the energy with which he
adapted to the theories of color which
were propagated by Robert Delaunay.
He brought to the exploitation of
Delaunay's theories a largeness of
feeling which can truly be called
American; and after years of careful
study he was able to use color, in itself
and by itself, to blast off into an
empyrean of his own devising. While
still adhering to what he called "the
fundamental laws of composition
(placements and displacements of mass
as in the human body in movement)"
he avoided all direct reference to
identifiable forms; the soft voluptuous
shapes floated freely, as here, defining
and redefining themselves in terms of
pure color.

5. Arthur G. Dove
Nature Symbolized, No. 2, 1911
The Art Institute of Chicago

Dove was neither learned nor widely traveled, but by 1911 he was able to symbolize the forces of Nature as vividly as any of his contemporaries in Germany or elsewhere. With highly energized tusk-and-comma forms he could epitomize the look of an upland landscape traversed by high winds, marked out alternately by sun and shadow, sharply accented by hillock and tall tree.

6. Georgia O'Keeffe
Evening Star III, 1917
The Museum of Modern Art, New York

At the time of her New York debut in 1916 Georgia O'Keeffe already had at her command a highly simplified vocabulary of form. With just one or two shapes, sumptuous in color and dreamlike in the way that they oozed slowly across the paper, she produced images which were peculiar to herself. They might be, as here, a portrait of Nature at her most hushed and velvety; but they were also fragments of autobiography that stood, as she said herself, for "things that I had no words for."

culed the honest-workman approach to art which was common among the French painters of his acquaintance. In 1909 he was having every possible success in France as a late-Impressionist painter, only to decide from one day to the next that he couldn't be bothered to go on with it. *French Impetuosity* was the title he gave to one of his later paintings, and in New York he lived up to it. New Yorkers took to him at once, and they were relieved to find at the Armory Show that in his hands even Cubism took on a jazzy, accessible character. He identified very strongly with America, and he was serious enough to realize from his daily contacts with the Stieglitz circle that New York would soon have an avant-garde that would not have to depend on injections of new blood from abroad.

Duchamp had always liked and admired Picabia. As the youngest son of a French provincial lawyer, Duchamp had been reared in a tradition of thrift, hard work and systematic consolidation. Picabia had a recklessness, a wide and exotic social acquaintance, and an iconoclastic, spendthrift turn of mind which were a revelation to Duchamp when the two first became friends in the fall of 1911. He just hadn't thought it possible that such people existed. Picabia by the spring of 1913 had become so much a New Yorker by adoption that Duchamp was beyond doubt wide open to suggestion when Walter Pach, coorganizer of the Armory Show, proposed in the winter of 1914–15 that he, too, should cross the Atlantic. Duchamp had been excused from military service because of a weak heart. He was bored by the

7. Marsden Hartley
Portrait of a German Officer, 1914
The Metropolitan Museum of Art, New York

In his middle 30s Marsden Hartley spent much of his time in Europe. Stieglitz paid for him to go to Paris in 1912, and in 1913–14 he was in Munich and came to know Kandinsky and his colleagues in the Blue Rider group. Having seen

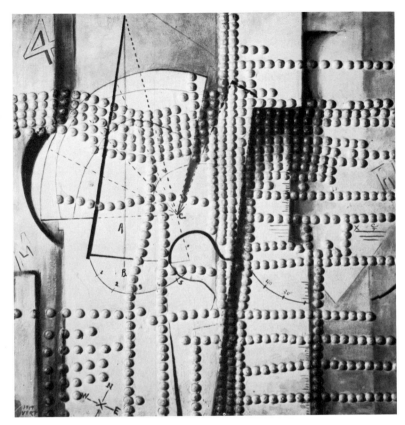

8. John R. Covert
Time, 1919
Yale University Art Gallery,
　New Haven, Conn.

Among the Americans who looked closely at both Duchamp and Picabia during World War I was John Covert. In his abstract collages there are echoes, for instance, of Duchamp's use of string in *Chocolate Grinder No. 2* of 1914 (fig. 18) and of Picabia's equivocal way with machine forms. There was no lasting drive to Covert's art, and before long he gave up and went into business; but that an American should have made such pieces as *Time* at that moment in history is an indication of the spread of avant-garde ideas after World War I.

the German military machine at close quarters, he was able in his *Portrait of a German Officer* to suggest to what an extent the uniform was the man. The little picture also demonstrates the uses of a pictorial shorthand in which shapes are abstracted from nature and fitted together in such a way as to make an image as striking as it is concise.

10. Arthur G. Dove
*Portrait of
   Alfred Stieglitz,*
   1925
The Museum of Modern
   Art, New York

9. Morton Schamberg
God, c. 1918
Philadelphia Museum of Art

With miter box and a plumbing trap, Morton Schamberg in 1918 fabricated an object which can stand as a symbol of imperious masculinity: an unbeliever's view of Jehovah which after more than half a century still looks modern.

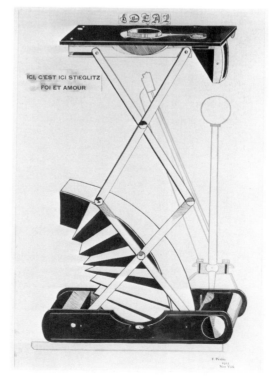

To Picabia in 1915 (*below right*) and to Arthur Dove (*above right*) ten years later, it seemed natural to think of Stieglitz in terms of the camera which he used with such exemplary skill. These two ''portraits'' are portraits as much of the apparatus as of the man. Faith and love in the case of Picabia, the coiled spring in the case of Dove; these seemed to them indispensable to any true portrait of Stieglitz the artistic impresario and Stieglitz the photographer.

11. Francis Picabia
*Here, This
   Is Stieglitz,* 1915
The Metropolitan
   Museum of Art,
   New York

IV. Francis Picabia
I See Again in Memory My Dear Udnie,
1914
The Museum of Modern Art, New York

Like his close friend Marcel Duchamp,
Picabia liked to think of the human
anatomy in terms of emblematic
machinery. But whereas Duchamp took
great care to cover his tracks and to
present his findings in terms that were
close to abstraction, Picabia came out
into the open. This particular painting
was prompted by Picabia's admiration
for a dancer whom he had met on the
boat on his way to New York in 1913.
Petal-shapes, clearly expressive of
uplifted skirts, open themselves to
nozzle-like forms, no less clearly
expressive of the male sexual organ at a
moment of strenuous activity. Picabia
at that time owned Duchamp's *The
Bride* of 1912 (fig. 24), and there are
evident affinities between the two.

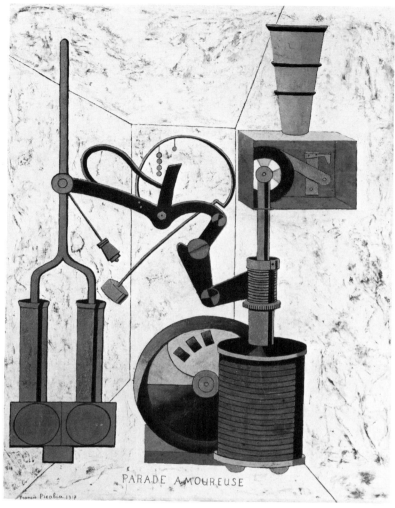

12. Francis Picabia
Amorous Parade, 1917
Mr. and Mrs. Morton G. Neumann, Chicago

Picabia was as ready to laugh at himself as he was to laugh at everyone else, and in this painting the rituals of seduction are turned into something that is not only graceless but inherently ludicrous.

13. Man Ray
Interior, 1915
Philadelphia Museum of Art

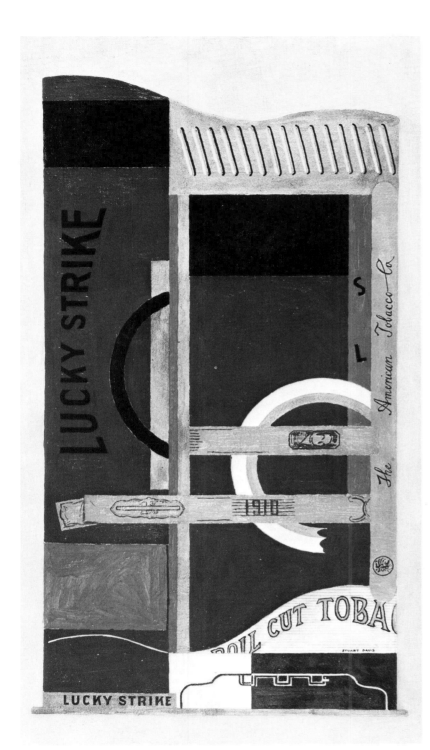

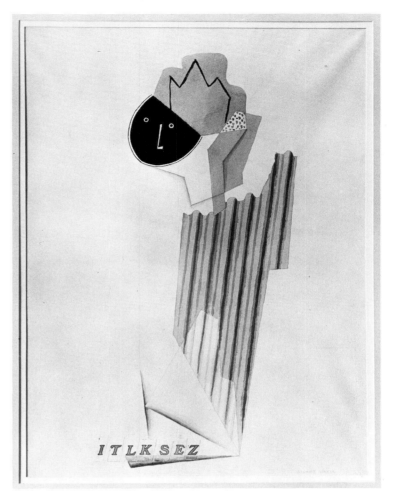

14. (*left*) Stuart Davis
Lucky Strike, 1921
The Museum of Modern Art, New York

15. (*above*) Stuart Davis
Itlksez, 1921
Lane Foundation, Leominster, Mass.

Stuart Davis was an inspiration to other American artists for the best part of half a century. His open mind, his readiness to work hard and long to realize his own nature, his determination that his art should relate to the here and now of America—all these were key traits in the development of an independent American art. In *Lucky Strike* he took a familiar commercial image and used it as the basis of a fastidious hand-crafted contribution to the art of the day.

seedy, depleted, unsmiling character of Parisian art life in war-time. He took the boat for New York in June, 1915, and he lived there, on and off, until his death in 1968.

Duchamp at that time was known to thousands of Americans as "the man who painted the *Nude Descending a Staircase*" (Volume 5). That painting had been beyond question the great success of the Armory Show. It had been lampooned and caricatured day after day in the newspapers; it had been bought, sight unseen, by telegram from Albuquerque; at the Armory itself the crowd around it was so thick that many visitors never got to see it at all. Duchamp in 1915 had a celebrity in North America which he was never to acquire in the country of his birth. Walter Pach was at the dock when he arrived. They went straight to Walter Arensberg's apartment at 33 West 67th Street, and Duchamp stayed there not for an afternoon but for a month. Unlike Picabia, he had no visible needs, was not interested in possessions, and never put himself forward. But when it became clear that he had no new paintings to sell and that even to breathe the air of New York cost money, it was John Quinn above all who came to the rescue. Quinn was not rich by the standards of a Mellon or a Morgan, but when it came to man-to-man patronage he did more for art and literature in our century than anyone, anywhere. If it had not been for John Quinn, it is quite possible that T. S. Eliot would never have completed *The Waste Land* nor James Joyce seen *Ulysses* in the bookstores. Ezra Pound and Joseph Conrad were among the others who had reason to be grateful to Quinn; and when Quinn sensed that Marcel Duchamp could use a little money he hired him, part-time and with all possible discretion, to look after his French correspondence for an honorarium of $100 a month. With this, Duchamp could live as he liked to live and get on with his work.

What work? Duchamp in that respect was the opposite of his close friend Picabia. Picabia had the instincts of a top-class vaudeville performer. He liked to "make it new" continually, and he liked his ideas to get across on the instant. Where living was

16. Arthur G. Dove
The Intellectual, 1925
The Museum of Modern Art, New York

Arthur Dove was a master of the symbolic portrait. Here the dried bones of the nose and mouth, the vast round cranium which is simulated by an empty plate, and the pocket balance which sits where the heart should be—all add up to a concise portrait of the intellectual as desiccated calculating machine.

14

V. Francis Picabia
Very Rare Picture Upon the Earth, 1915
Peggy Guggenheim Foundation,
  Venice

Épreuve d'artiste 1/10   *Jacques Villon*

17. Jacques Villon
Marcel Duchamp, 1953
The Museum of Modern Art, New York

Jacques Villon was one of the finest etchers of this century; in this portrait of his younger brother Marcel Duchamp, he combined close personal knowledge with a rare technical elegance.

concerned, Duchamp learned a great deal from Picabia, but all his life he was indifferent to direct contact with the public. If anything, he disliked the idea of the work of art as something that could be comprehended directly and instantaneously. He was insistent that the enormous work on which he had been engaged since 1912 was not "a picture" in the traditional sense and that immediate retinal effect was not its aim. Painting since Courbet had gone steadily downhill, in his view, by substituting retinal satisfaction—the "pleasures of the eye"—for the more complex mingling of image and idea, delectation and close study, which gives true dignity to art.

This meant that the Duchamp who disembarked in New York in June, 1915, was no longer, in any but a historical sense, "the man who painted the *Nude Descending*." He had decided to demystify the act of painting, with its patient handcrafting, its pervasive smell of turpentine, and its courtship of the eye. New ways of conjugating experience were at hand, and it was for the artist to make use of them. A work of art was not simply something to look at; it was also, and much more, something to think about. And the way to force people to think about it was to take it out of the traditional contexts of art.

All this meant a break with art, as it was then understood (and nowhere more so than in Duchamp's family circle, where just about everyone was an artist and the theory, practice and politics of art were continually to the fore). Whether or not the break was prompted in part by a period of intense private emotion is a matter over which controversy has waxed hot and shows no signs of waning. But in any case Duchamp was, like everyone else, a product of his time. He grew up at a time when there seemed to be no limit to the number of ways in which machines could change life for the better. Machines made fresh miracles every day. And it seemed to Duchamp that the taut, impersonal procedures of the machine could also be carried over into art, and above all into the archaic procedures of freehand drawing. ("An absolutely precise coordinate drawing, with no relation to arty handwork," was his own description for what he was after at that time.)

In the late fall of 1911 Duchamp had been with Apollinaire and Picabia to see a stage production in Paris of Raymond Roussel's *Impressions of Africa*; in October, 1912, he made a motor trip from Paris to the Jura mountains, again with Apollinaire and Picabia. These were two capital experiences for him. From the Roussel he got a reinforced delight in the possibilities of the pun as a poetic instrument; he also got the notion, mooted in passing by Roussel, of a painting-machine which would put the honest workmen of the Salons out of business. During the journey to the

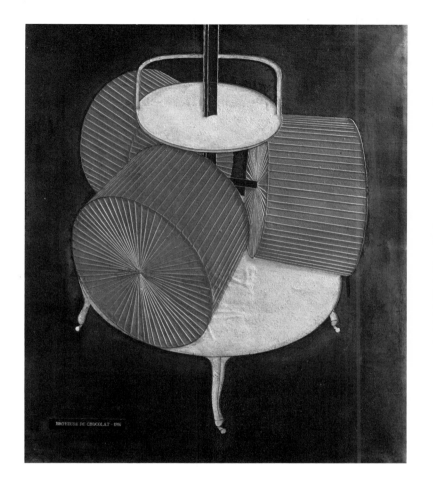

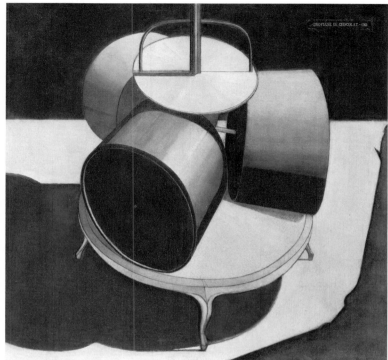

18. (*left*) Marcel Duchamp
Chocolate Grinder, No. 2, 1914
Philadelphia Museum of Art

19. (*above*) Marcel Duchamp
Chocolate Grinder, No. 1, 1913
Philadelphia Museum of Art

In Duchamp's progress from conventional painting to something more like map- or diagram-making an important part was played by a chocolate grinder which he had seen in the window of the best confectioner in Rouen. Initially in 1913 he produced a traditional still-life painting (*No. 1*) varied only by the application of a leather label in the upper right-hand corner. Then in 1914 he produced an entirely different version (*No. 2*) in which the image was built rather than painted—and built quite frankly in three dimensions, with an emphatic use of glued string to make it clear that this was not "a painting," in the standard sense, but a constructed object of a new kind.

Jura it undoubtedly became clear to him that Picabia fantasized about the motorcar-as-sexual-partner in ways now familiar to the point of tedium but then quite new; and from the notes which he later published we know that Duchamp took his habitual, detached but very incisive interest in the metaphoric possibilities of every aspect of the automobile, from the imperious silver-mounted headlamp to the lowly and fallible intestinal piping. Machines of one sort or another were to form the basic set on which many of his ideas would be structured. The machine did not serve him as a metaphor for limitless power and impeccable functioning. He saw it, rather, as a metaphor for frustration, discomfiture, pointless effort, self-deception and the failure to communicate. Duchamp was both skeptic and ironist; it was not in his nature to bow down to the machine. But from the time (November–December, 1911) when he painted a little picture of a coffee mill for his brother's kitchen, he was always aware of the

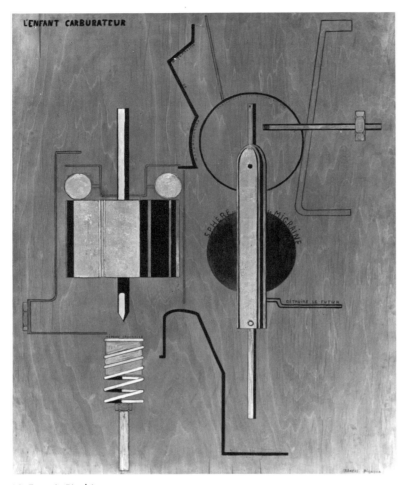

20. Francis Picabia
The Child Carburetor, c. 1919
The Solomon R. Guggenheim Museum, New York

By 1919 Picabia was fully cognizant of Duchamp's infinitely complex adaptation (in the *Large Glass*) of the machine aesthetic to the vagaries of erotic emotion. His *The Child Carburetor* is based on a cross-section of an actual carburetor; but in transferring it to canvas Picabia introduced a whole series of allusions, by turns droll and wry, to the ins and outs of our most intimate experiences.

21. Francis Picabia
The Blessed Virgin, 1920
Reproduced in *391*, Paris,
no. 12, March, 1920

By nominating an ink blot for serious consideration as a work of art, and by giving it a blasphemous subtitle, Picabia scored twice over in Dada terms.

22. (*below*) Man Ray
Rrose Sélavy
(*Portrait of Marcel Duchamp*),
1923
Private collection, New York

When Duchamp began to produce readymades he decided to take a pseudonym as remote as possible from his own name. Taking the most ordinary girl's name he could think of—"if I wanted to give my daughter the worst possible name I'd choose Rose"—he went on to take as his surname "Sélavy" (a phonetic rendering of *C'est la vie*, "That's life!" in French), and Rose Sélavy he remained in one work after another. In 1923 Man Ray added a real-life rose and a punning form of the name to this portrait, which emphasizes an androgynous element in Duchamp's features.

machine's implications. The coffee mill in question had the unassuming look of a household pet, and it was still very painterly in its execution. But it stood for the analysis of a machine in movement; it stood for the diagram as opposed to the freehand drawing; and in a very discreet way it stood for the compulsive grinding which precedes the sexual climax. And it hung, like a ticking bomb, in one of the headquarters of Parisian retinal painting.

Duchamp was a child of his time in other ways too. His favorite books were the ones which had come out just before he himself was born, in July, 1887. "Rimbaud and Lautréamont seemed too old for me," he said later. "I wanted something younger."

"Something younger" meant the Symbolist poet Jules Laforgue, whose two books of poems came out in 1885 and 1886; from Laforgue, Duchamp got the initial motif for his *Nude Descending*. (At a time when the traditional myths have lost most of their interest for artists and nonartists alike, the mythology of sexual pursuit and conquest has retained its fascination intact.) It also meant Mallarmé: the Spanish-language poet Octavio Paz is certainly right in associating the downward march of Duchamp's *Nude* to "the solemn moment" at which "Mallarmé's Igitur abandons his room forever and goes step by step down the stairs which lead to the crypt of his ancestors." "Something younger" meant finally Villiers de l'Isle Adam's novel *Eve of the Future* (1886). It could be a coincidence, but it would be a pretty big one, that Duchamp worked for 12 years—1912–23—on his *Large Glass,* which, like *Eve of the Future,* has to do with the subjection of the male to a female of more than normal authority and power. Duchamp was born in the heyday of Symbolism and he remained a symbolist all his life: a poet, that is to say, who produced complex and evocative images which every generation reinterprets for itself.

That was the background of the man who, from 1912 onward, abandoned easel painting. Thereafter he produced, on the one hand, a small number of concise, irreducible, nonrepeatable statements; on the other, he made a sustained attempt, on the scale of epic, to reconcile image and idea. His immediate impact in New York was substantial, but it was not owed so much to individual works of art as to the elegance with which he questioned the hierarchies of art. Those hierarchies had to do, broadly speaking, with the mastery of two interdependent elements: emotive subject matter, to begin with, and a force of expression which could challenge comparison with the great achievements of the past. That was the basis on which Cézanne's *Grandes Baigneuses* (Volume 1) and Matisse's *Joy of Life* (Volume 2) and Picasso's *Les Demoiselles d'Avignon* (Volume 4) were ranked where they were: at the top. They were "modern," but they also brought with them a long baggage-train of memory, and association, and affections asked for and readily granted.

When Duchamp began to produce what were later called his "readymades," he didn't want anything like that. He went to great pains to nominate objects to which it was impossible to have an aesthetic reaction: a bottle rack, for instance. "My choice," he said later, "was always based on visual indifference and a total absence of taste, either bad or good." In the precursor of the readymades, the *Bicycle Wheel* of 1913 (fig. 23), he took a bicycle wheel and put it, fork upward, on top of a stool. The wheel still spins, but it has been taken out of the context in which

23. Marcel Duchamp
Bicycle Wheel (1951
 third version after lost original of 1913)
The Museum of Modern Art, New York

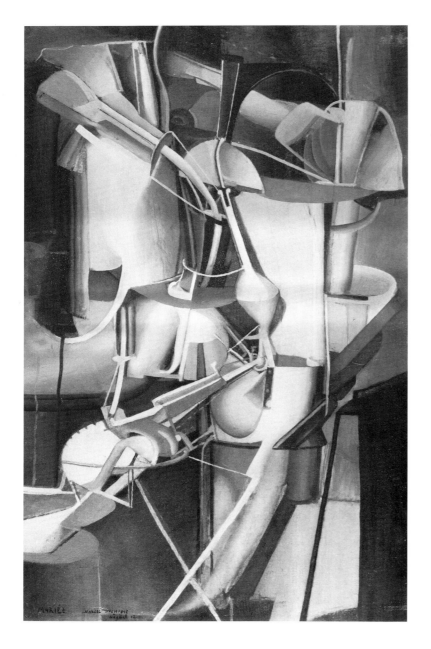

24. (*left*) Marcel Duchamp
The Bride, 1912
Philadelphia Museum of Art

25. (*above*) Gustave Courbet
The Robing of the Bride, 1865–70
Smith College Museum of Art, Northampton, Mass.

we normally expect to see it. The same thing happened with the snow shovel which was the first readymade to be produced in New York, and with the comb, the urinal, the typewriter cover, the hat rack and the coat rack, which in the same way were nominated as readymades during Duchamp's first years there.

People have for so long been conditioned to think of new art in terms of scandal that it is worth saying here that Duchamp did not do these things to shock, or to annoy, but simply to investigate the nature of art and of our responses to it. He did not bring the bicycle wheel into the living room in order to be provocative but because he liked it. "To see that wheel turning," he said to the art dealer Arturo Schwarz, "was very soothing, very comforting, a sort of opening of avenues on to other things than the material life of every day. . . . I enjoyed looking at it, just as I enjoy looking at the flames dancing in a fireplace." This was, quite genuinely and without affectation of any sort, the alternative art for which the times were calling; and it reminds us of something soon forgotten when the routines of taste take over—

In *The Bride* Duchamp carried the depersonalization of the human body just one stage further. Like *The Passage* (pl. VI) it was painted in Munich, at a time when the idea of the *Large Glass* (pl. VII) was in full germination. The female body is seen here both as a machine and as a vessel; the bride as engine room is its true subject, and there is no longer any trace of the hesitations and uncertainties which are traditionally associated with virginity.

that art does not lie only in the object perceived but also in the way we think of it. Duchamp liked to prove this by taking an object that was beyond the pale of established art and making it jump out of its class, as it were, either unaltered or with minimal interference from himself.

Once he himself had opted out of the fine-art context, Duchamp found that ideas came to him as fast as he could note them down. He became, in fact, a kind of reception center for notions outlawed by the conventions of modernist art. Among those which he put down on paper but never followed up are questions which half a century later were to preoccupy a whole generation of intelligent young people. What is the irreducible element in language? What would constitute a truly modern dictionary? How should an index of all knowledge be organized? To what extent can chance be given its freedom in the arts? Other ideas remained peculiar to himself. What are the verbal equivalents of colors that cannot be seen? Should not every government have its Ministry of Coincidences? On a more practical level, how can we get rid of oil paint on canvas as a way of producing images? Couldn't we use toothpaste on glass? Or brilliantine? Or cold cream? How would they last? (Not too well, apparently: Duchamp scrawled the words "not solid" at the bottom of that page.)

It was one of the many contradictory things about Duchamp that although he enjoyed making fun of the traditional solemnities of art, he also occupied himself twice over—from 1912 to 1923, and again from 1946 to 1966—with works of art as ambitious, and as elaborate, as any that we have seen in this century. But he produced them on his own terms, and in the case of the *Large Glass* he had in mind what he called "a marriage of mental and visual reactions." It was not enough to look at the *Large Glass* as one looks at a Titian or a Vermeer; the *Large Glass* was there to be *consulted,* rather as one consults an atlas: as a sign-system incomplete in itself. "The ideas in the *Glass,*" he said in 1959, "are more important than the visual realization"; and the ideas were contained on the 94 unnumbered pages of notes which were first published in 1934.

The *Large Glass* belongs, beyond question, to that select and daunting company of major works of art as to the understanding of which there can be no short cut. No single work of art produced in this century has been so closely studied or commented on at so great a length. None has prompted so wide a variety of interpretations, nearly all of them valid in some degree yet none of them definitive. What follows cannot pretend, therefore, to replace the extended studies of André Breton, Robert Lebel, Richard Hamilton, Octavio Paz and John Golding.

DUCHAMP AND THE DISROBING OF THE BRIDE

The full title of the *Large Glass* is *The Bride Stripped Bare by Her Bachelors, Even.* Like most of Duchamp's titles it has mischief in it. But it does, even so, hint at the fundamental subject matter of the work, which is the possession of one human being by another. Every society, and within our own society every generation, has its own way of ritualizing the robings and disrobings which this involves. (The *Large Glass* had, for instance, a particularly brilliant and hilarious contemporary in Stravinsky's *Les Noces,* which occupied the composer over exactly the same 12-year period, off and on, and takes us to the point at which, in classic accounts of matrimony, all is presumed to go well.) Duchamp never did anything without a reason, and as he believed that Courbet, in the 1850s and '60s, had set painting on the wrong path by placing too much emphasis on the physicality of the paint, it is quite possible that in part of the *Large Glass* he had it in mind to rephrase the subject matter of Courbet's *The Robing of the Bride* (fig. 25).

By choosing as his subject the overture to what is the most decisive single moment in most people's experience, Duchamp made sure that he would never lack an audience. From that point onward, however, he made things just about as difficult as he could, both for himself and for us. To the extent that he was a child of his time—a Frenchman born in 1887—he inherited a view of sexual activity which was pragmatic, ironical, uninhibited and dis-idealized. Among the Frenchmen of his age group, sex was a matter not of unfocused yearning but of fact: fact reconnoitered, fact evaluated, fact acted upon. All this lent itself very well to the mechanistic illustration, and Duchamp was by no means alone in seeing the machine both as an extension of human powers and as a commentary upon their shortcomings. Thus far, he ran with the winds then prevailing.

Duchamp in life laughed readily and with a most infectious enjoyment; and the subject of the *Large Glass* could be broken down in terms of a farce by Georges Feydeau (1862–1921), as great a master of theatrical contrivance as ever lived. We have only to think of the initial idea—nine Bachelors in pursuit of the same pretty girl—to see Feydeau's mind begin to race. No less provocative to Feydeau would have been the fact that the Bachelors are distinguished only by the molds into which the essence of their masculinity is to be poured. The uniform was the man, in each case, and they were not seen as individuals but as archetypes of the Policeman, the Undertaker, the Priest, the Delivery Boy, the Station Master.

Feydeau would have left us limp with laughter; but although

VI. Marcel Duchamp
*The Passage from the Virgin to the
    Bride,* 1912
The Museum of Modern Art, New York

During a visit to Munich in July/August, 1912, Duchamp made a drawing which he later identified as the "first sketch for 'The Bride Stripped Bare by the Bachelors.'" He also painted this picture which, as its title indicates, has likewise a hymeneal subject. That subject is treated, however, in a way which is partly mechanical and partly metaphysical. In other words the "passage" in question can be found in the female anatomy, and it is here shown in terms of machinery; but it also refers to the change of status which is implied in the condition of matrimony. The painting also has in it elements of the serial representation for which Duchamp became notorious at the time of his *Nude Descending a Staircase, No. 2* (Volume 5).

VII. Marcel Duchamp
*The Bride Stripped Bare by Her Bachelors, Even
 (Large Glass)*, 1915–23
Philadelphia Museum of Art

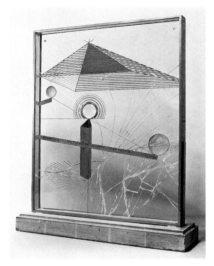

27. Marcel Duchamp
To Be Looked at with One Eye,
    Close to, for Almost an Hour, 1918
The Museum of Modern Art, New York

28. Marcel Duchamp
Fresh Widow, 1920
The Museum of Modern Art,
    New York

26. Marcel Duchamp
With Hidden Noise, 1916
Philadelphia Museum of Art

With this work Duchamp pioneered, as early as 1916, the notion of the poetic object, which was to play an important role in Surrealist activity in the 1920s and 30s. He also pioneered the idea of participation by others (in this case, his patron Walter Arensberg) in ways unknown to the initiator of the piece. Here a ball of twine is held firmly between two brass plates, which in their turn are kept in place by four long bolts. Inside the twine is a small object, chosen and placed by Arensberg, which makes a mysterious noise when the piece is shaken. Objects of everyday use are combined in a completely irrational or nonutilitarian way to produce something that we recognize as having a strange power and a presence all its own. That strangeness is compounded by the addition of a further, hidden element: a secret from which even the artist himself is excluded.

The *Large Glass* (pl. VII) is, apart from so much else, an inventory of bizarre and original technical procedures. Often these have a double and an ironical intention. *To Be Looked at* is, for instance, related to the section on the right-hand side of the lower panel of the *Large Glass* which is known as the "Oculist Witnesses." (It has, in particular, the same ingredient of "silver scratching" on glass.) Duchamp here refers to a scientific device which in everyday life serves to test the observer's eyesight; and he uses it to make the conventional art lover adjust in response to a shift in visual language and, no less importantly, to a shift in pace (whence the mischievous title of this work).

Duchamp loved puns, both verbal and visual. The title of *Fresh Widow* combines the notions of (i) a French window, (ii) a woman recently and still deeply bereft and (iii) a widow already eager for masculine attentions. "Fresh," "French," "window" and "widow" form, that is to say, a kind of verbal conglomerate, which we may assemble as we think fit. In visual terms, what we see is a window in mourning: a standard French frame in which eight panels of polished black leather have been substituted for clear glass. The black has obvious overtones of widowhood—the "panes" could be there to protect the mourner from the curiosity of passers-by—but Duchamp wanted a high polish on the black leather, so that it could also seem that we are looking out, as we look out in times of mourning, upon nothingness.

there are some very funny things about the *Large Glass* it is a great deal more than a metaphor, however ingenious, for the discomfitures which come about when young men pursue a pretty girl and don't quite get her. There is something awesome about the *Large Glass,* and that awesomeness does not relate only to its prodigious complication. The *Large Glass* has something to tell us, but to take possession of that something is almost as difficult as for the Bachelors to take possession of the Bride. The *Glass* works on many levels, and to concentrate on any one of them is to let the others slip out of focus. To see the truth of this, we have only to look at one of the many pictures by Picabia which, between 1915 and 1919, ran parallel to one or another of Duchamp's preoccupations. A Picabia of that date works perfectly, on the scale of epigram and on one level at a time. Himself a satyr in the prime of life, Picabia was both funny and direct in his treatment of sexual subjects. He stands before us as a practiced man of the world who is intelligent enough to abstract just one element at a time from what Duchamp is doing, and he brings that one element into sharp focus, on its own.

But with Duchamp nothing is ever quite, or ever only, what it seems. It is possible, for instance, to read the general layout of the *Large Glass* in terms of Christian iconography; the upper half then becomes a variant of the Apotheosis of the Virgin, while the lower half is given over to terrestrial concerns. But Duchamp also sanctioned a purely secular reading in which the theme of the Bride was prompted by the memory of the fairgrounds of his youth, where the public was invited to throw wooden balls at a pair of dolls which represented a bride and groom. In that case, according to Octavio Paz, "the Bride is a doll; the people who throw the balls are her Bachelors; the Oculist Witnesses are the public; the top inscription is the scoreboard." In the isolation of the Bride and in the fact that the Bachelors are seen to huddle together, set apart in their turn by the fact of being in uniform, there can equally well be seen an appeal to ancestral memory: to the cult of an unattainable womanhood, and to the mingling of terror and excitement with which the male animal stands on the threshold of manhood.

In these matters we all of us negotiate from strength in some areas and from weakness in others; that is one reason for the fascination of the *Glass.* But what if it secretes yet other levels of meaning? What if it is a metaphor for the renewal of language and for the possibility of completely new modes of communication? What if even the curiously dry, impersonal, nonassociative color had a meaning beyond the fact that Duchamp wanted to avoid the color structures of conventional art?

In his rejection of conventional art Duchamp did, in effect,

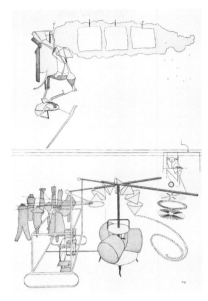

29. Marcel Duchamp
The Large Glass Completed,
1965–66
Galleria Schwarz Collection, Milan

In 1965 Duchamp was persuaded to give an indication of how the *Large Glass* (pl. VII) might have looked if he had gone all the way with his original schema. This etching resulted; it is of great historic interest, as being our only precise diagrammatic record of Duchamp's intentions.

impose upon himself year upon year of technical experimentation. He wanted to invent methods of image-making to which the concept of taste could not apply, any more than it applied to engineering drawings or to the color of the liquids in a drugstore window. (It took many months, for instance, to decide exactly how dust could be incorporated into the *Large Glass* as a material like any other.) In its use of lead, lead wire, silver foil, and perspective drawing of a minutely scientific sort, the *Large Glass* is not in the least like any other work of art. Yet the virtuosity is never there for its own sake: it is fundamental both to the thing seen and the thing thought about.

There are many aspects of the *Glass* over which controversy is still very much alive. We have to consider, for instance, the extent to which Duchamp meant to introduce into the *Glass* the concept of the fourth dimension, so much talked of in Paris at that time. He had been at great pains to reinvent, almost, the idea of the third dimension as it was elucidated by classical perspective. Was it because he believed that, as John Golding has put it, "three-dimensional objects could be considered as the flat shadows or reflections of the fourth dimension, invisible because it could never be seen by the human eye"? Was the *Large Glass* a projection of a four-dimensional object: "the apparition of an appearance"? On that reading, the ostensible subject of the *Glass,* with its bawdy, turn-of-the-century implications, would be no more than a bait to draw us into an adventure of quite another kind.

The exact nature of the mechanical implications of the *Glass* is also very far from having been decided once and for all. Undeniably Duchamp was much impressed by the motor trip which he and Apollinaire took with Picabia in October, 1912; and when they all got back from the Jura mountains, Duchamp projected a large-scale work in which the protagonist would be an automobile: "the machine with 5 hearts, the pure child of nickel and platinum which must dominate the Paris–Jura road." The motorcar was personified in all this as "the girl born without a mother." It had a father-inventor, or an inventor-father, but it was generated independently of the female womb; there was an echo in this of the ancient alchemists' belief that when the alchemical formula was put into action a motherless child could be created.

Duchamp himself said that if he referred to alchemy in the *Glass,* it was "in the only way in which one can use alchemy nowadays—without knowing it." But there are many arcane references in the *Glass* which may or may not be there by accident. The subject itself, to begin with, can be interpreted in alchemical terms. In 1968 Pontus Hulten, director of the Moderna Museet in Stockholm, took up a point first made by his compatriot Ulf Linde: that the disrobing of the bride was likened by the philosopher Solidonius to the way in which the material used by the alchemists lost all its color in the process of liquefaction and transmutation.

The *Large Glass* can be read, therefore, in terms of the "philosophical marriage" through which the alchemist aimed to produce gold. The marriage in question involved "the baser, dry, male element, sulphur" and "the volatile female element, mercury." Hulten goes on, "The generative operation took place within a 'cosmic oven,' whose lower and upper parts were respectively male and female; the mercury was contained in a vessel of pure glass—a metaphor often applied to the Virgin. It seems likely that the upper part of Duchamp's *Large Glass* relates to the philosopher's mercury, which is the principle both of the universal love of nature and of redemption through work; while the lower part, the Bachelor's apparatus, is connected with the alchemical concept of sulphur."

Duchamp's notional Minister of Coincidences might intervene at this point and say that when Duchamp was first working seriously on the *Glass,* in Munich in 1912, he had at hand one of the world's great alchemical libraries. Whether or not he ever went there, the alchemical interpretation of the *Glass* should be taken seriously, along with the automobilist interpretation, the symbolist interpretation, the interpretation from speculative geometry, and half a dozen others. If there is in more than one of them an element of lunatic proliferation, that is in the nature of the game that the *Glass* plays with us. The stakes are high, and the wins and losses absolute.

The *Glass* is quintessentially modern, in that Duchamp is both the protagonist, the man who charts the work's progress in a spirit of total commitment, and the ironical spectator who continually asks himself, "What is a picture really for? What are we doing here that could not be done elsewhere? What are the new kinds of involvement that art has yet to bestow upon us?" Octavio Paz put this point to perfection when he wrote in 1969 that the *Glass* is both a contribution to mythology and a criticism of it. "I am reminded," he said, "of *Don Quixote,* which is both an epic novel and a criticism of the epic. It is with creations such as *Don Quixote* that modern irony was born; with Duchamp, and with other poets of the 20th century such as Joyce and Kafka, the irony turns against itself. The circle closes; it is the end of one epoch and the beginning of another." Once again it turns out that the *Glass* is always up-to-date. Where other classics of the early 20th century are already set fast in history, the *Glass* presents itself over and over again as the newest thing. Our own time is likely, for instance, to appear to posterity as the heyday of methodology: the moment at which method was accepted as the key to all things. If this is so, posterity will also remember what Octavio Paz said of the *Glass* that "what it gives us is the *spirit of the age:* Method, the critical Idea at the moment when it is meditating on itself, and when it reflects itself in the transparent nothingness of a pane of glass."

The *Large Glass* is the masterpiece of alternative art. And it puts forward a true alternative: one which remakes the experience of art. But it was not at all typical of alternative art. Duchamp never tangled with Authority, for example. He worked slowly and tenaciously, and in conditions of security. He had no thought of sounding an alarm or setting the world to rights. His work was rarely seen and almost never written about. (The first serious study of the *Large Glass,* by André Breton, was not published till 1935.) Though outwardly a big-city man, and everywhere the most welcome of guests, he worked like a hermit in the desert: apart and alone.

By contrast, alternative art in Europe was often in trouble with the law: exhibitions were shut down, meetings ended in dis-

VIII. Marcel Duchamp
Apolinère Enameled (Girl with Bedstead), 1916–17
Philadelphia Museum of Art

Duchamp delighted in what he called "corrected readymades": objects which
he could transform with a minimum of embellishment. In this case a reference
to the poet Apollinaire has been grafted onto an advertisement for Sapolin
Enamel. It is typical of Duchamp's delicate fancy that the grafting might seem
to have been done by the little girl in the advertisement itself before she moved
on to enamel the bedstead in the picture below.

27

30. Marcel Duchamp
Why Not Sneeze, Rose Sélavy? (1964
replica of original of 1921)
The Museum of Modern Art, New York

For multiple incongruity, *Why Not Sneeze* has few rivals in the history of the Surrealist object. Not only are its ingredients dreamlike in their improbability but in one important case their physical appearance is deceptive. (What we take to be lumps of sugar are, in fact, lumps of marble, so the piece is much heavier than it looks.) Throughout the 1920s and early 30s imaginations were put to work to invent disquieting conjunctions of everyday objects; but first prize still goes to Duchamp's bird cage, with its cargo of marble sugar, thermometer and cuttlefish bone.

order, magazines were suppressed, prosecutions were initiated. Much art was improvised in times of national emergency and had, quite naturally, a frantic last-minute look. The economics of starvation dictated its materials, as often as not. Much of it was backed by a rudimentary but untiring publicity machine of a kind from which Duchamp held aloof. Under the generic name of Dada it was a rackety, pugnacious, many-sided and almost entirely subversive activity. And yet Duchamp turns out to have been perpetual president of the whole adventure, in ways which are still being deciphered. European Dada arose from a specific historical and geographical situation; and Duchamp for most of

its life was 3,000 and more miles away. But it now seems as if the Dada group, like the Bachelors in the *Large Glass,* were poured into molds of Duchamp's devising.

THE SCENE IN ZURICH

Duchamp was fascinated by chance. As much as any of his works, he liked the *Three Standard Stoppages* of 1913–14 (fig. 31), which was based on a chance operation: the outline of three threads, each one meter long, dropped from a height of one meter onto a canvas painted Prussian blue. It amused him very

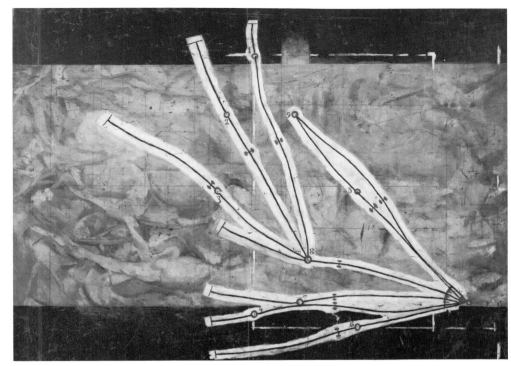

31. Marcel Duchamp
Three Standard Stoppages, 1913–14
The Museum of Modern Art, New York

32. Marcel Duchamp
Network of Stoppages, 1914
The Museum of Modern Art, New York

Network of Stoppages is an example of the manifold ways in which Duchamp in 1914 was edging away from conventional painting and toward the procedures of the *Large Glass* (pl. VII). It consists of three superimposed compositions. Underneath, and laid on its side, is an unfinished painting of a young man and a girl in a landscape. This relates to a painting which Duchamp made in 1911 as a wedding present for his sister Suzanne. By demoting it here to the status almost of a scratch pad, Duchamp says a brisk "goodbye" to conventional painting.
What looks like a conscientiously drawn map on top of the painting is

in fact a pencil layout, half the final size, of the *Large Glass*. On top of this layout is a plan view of part of the left-hand side of the lower half of the *Large Glass*. This includes nine numbered circles which indicate the position of the molds into which the essence of the masculinity of the bachelors is to be poured. It should be added that although Duchamp had come to scorn traditional painting, the projection onto the glass of this complex series of interrelating units is an ideal demonstration of the strictest possible classical perspective.

much to build an elaborate structure around these random marks, just as it also amused him to start from a ready-made verbal statement and gently take it apart, as happened in the piece called *Apolinère Enameled* of 1916–17 (pl. VIII). He gave such things an overlay of meaning upon meaning that was all his own, but the basic ambition had a wide currency at the time. In Zürich, it was taken for granted among the writers and artists who formed from 1916 onward the Dada group that the liberation of

chance was one of the best things that had come out of the new century. "Chance appeared to us as a magical procedure by which we could transcend the barriers of causality and conscious volition, and by which the inner ear and eye became more acute. . . . For us, chance was the unconscious mind,' which Freud had discovered in 1900." The voice here is that of Hans Richter, painter, collagist, photographer and filmmaker, but the opinions are those of the Zürich Dada group as a whole. Dada

IX. Jean (Hans) Arp
Forest, 1916
Penrose Collection, London

X. Francis Picabia
Plumes, c. 1923–27?
Galleria Schwarz Collection, Milan

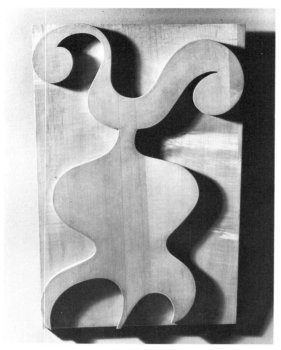

33. Jean (Hans) Arp
*Madame Torso with
a Wavy Hat*, 1916
Kunstmuseum, Bern

34. Jean (Hans) Arp
*Squares Arranged
According to the
Laws of Chance*,
1917
The Museum
of Modern Art,
New York

was not, strictly speaking, an art movement—in fact, it stood for the repudiation and abolition of art—and its energies related for the most part to poetry, typography, public relations and an idiosyncratic sub-species of the performing arts. Nurtured in a neutral country and galvanized by occasional visits by Picabia, Zürich Dada established prototypes of avant-garde activity which have still to be superseded: among them café-theater, the mixed-media happening, concrete poetry, automatic writing, and the use of aleatory procedures in art, poetry and music. When the Rumanian poet Tristan Tzara composed a Dada poem he would cut up newspaper articles into tiny fragments, shake them up in a bag, and scatter them across the table. As they fell, they made the poem; little further work was called for. When Jean Arp, the German-born sculptor–poet, tore up a drawing in despair and threw it on the studio floor he realized after a time that that, too, was a perfectly valid way to start a picture. And in 1917 Arp got into the habit of closing his eyes, underlining words or sentences in the newspaper with a pencil, and going on from there to write a complete poem. "A sentence from a newspaper gripped us as much as one from a prince among poets," he wrote in 1953.

Implicit in all this was contempt for the discredited bourgeois society which had allowed language to be debased by the mendacities of wartime and art to become a matter of routine. "In that wonderful Dada time," Arp wrote later, "we hated and despised finicky, laborious habits of work. We couldn't stand the other-worldly look of the 'titans' as they wrestled with problems of the spirit." Oil painting, in particular, had a rough ride with Dada. "When closely and sharply examined, the most perfect picture"—Arp is again the speaker—"is a warty, threadbare approximation, a dry porridge, a dismal moon-crater landscape." History has not always been kind to the Dadaists, and much of what they did now looks what they least wanted it to be: arty. In Zürich particularly the fact of Swiss neutrality makes the big talkers seem, in retrospect, both sheltered and effete. What still commands our respect is the constructive element; and that was provided by artists who would have come through in any case. Arp spoke for them when he said later that "we were looking for an art based on fundamentals, one which would cure the madness of the age. We wanted a new order of things to restore the balance between heaven and hell. Something told us that power-crazed gangsters would one day use art itself as a way of deadening men's minds."

It was a formidable program. Arp's work has survived not so much for its specifically Dada qualities as because he was equipped by his heredity, and by several years of intensive solitary effort, to decide for himself in which directions art needed to go. Born and reared in Strasbourg he had, like Strasbourg itself, a dual nationality. (Strasbourg, by turns French and German for centuries, was German till 1919, and French thereafter.) Arp for years called himself Hans Arp when in Germany and Jean Arp when in France; and in all his activities there was a mingling of German lyricism with down-to-earth French logical analysis. This paladin of modernity never lost the hot line to the German Middle Ages which he had acquired in first youth from a prolonged study of *Des Knaben Wunderhorn,* the anthology of German folksongs which had been published by Brentano and von Arnim in 1805–08. But at a very early age Arp became acquainted with Robert and Sonia Delaunay in Paris, and with Kandinsky and his friends in Munich, and with Herwarth Walden, the editor of *Der Sturm* in Berlin. By 1914 he was a valued though still youthful member of the pacific International: the gifted group who believed that creativity made nonsense of nationalism. And what he did under the aegis of Dada was, largely, to go on as before. There is an obvious contradiction between the grandiose program of Dada and the sweet good taste which is uppermost in the so-called Dada collages of Arp. In his painted wooden reliefs of the same period he indulged a play instinct which, once again, has nothing to do with an aesthetic of desperation. But the point of these beguiling little works is that they reintroduce into serious art a repertory of forms for which Cubism had had no place. Whimsy of a superior kind stood behind the shorthand ideograms for "bird," "forest," "water" and "human being"; and the shorthand in question was expressed in biomorphic terms. Arp's floppy, jokey, wayward, curvilinear forms took the stress out of art at a time when the major Cubists were mostly off duty and it had become clear that art was in need of an alternative formal alphabet. In his case, that alphabet was in the service of a relaxed humor; but over the next 50 or 60 years it was destined to run the whole gamut of human expression.

It was fundamental to an alternative art that magic could be made from the humblest of materials. "We 'painted,'" said one of the pioneers of Zürich Dada, "with scissors, adhesive plaster, sacking, paper." In Zürich this sprang from a conscious polemical preference; but the time was approaching when art would simply be compelled, in a defeated Germany, to work from an aesthetic of scarcity—in other words, with just about anything that came to hand. This applied as much to artists like Kurt Schwitters, who stood aloof from politics, as to those who stood for a committed point of view. If magic was made in Cologne, in Hanover and in Berlin, it was because artists were able to release the buried life within disregarded materials, just as Duchamp had released the buried life within the bicycle wheel.

As with Duchamp, language played its part in all this: sometimes in caption form, sometimes by unexpected conjugations of printed matter which made the observer jump back and forth between the act of looking and the act of reading. Duchamp had raided both domains in a spirit of detached inquiry; but German Dada was carried on in a society that was teetering toward total collapse. It was the work of men with nothing to lose, and its notional trajectory was not at all that of the traditional work of art: dealer → collector → museum. Its life span was estimated as nearer to that of the newspaper, or the public meeting, or the telegram marked "Urgent." Its function was to negotiate with chaos for terms of truce. It borrowed from the techniques of the handbill and the sticker, and it counted on the cooperation of observers whose situation was so desperate that they just couldn't afford not to understand. We should remember this when we try to imagine how the steeplechase of image and idea must have looked to those who had run it in the heyday (1919–22) of German Dada.

German Dada had nothing but the name in common with Zürich Dada. Fundamentally, Zürich Dada was a sub-department of the entertainment industry. Genuine revolution was not to be expected from evenings on which the young Arthur Rubinstein played the piano music of Saint-Saëns, and other performers evoked the Parisian *café-chantant* as it had been in the lifetime of Toulouse-Lautrec. "In Zürich," Richard Hülsenbeck wrote later, "people lived as they would have lived in a health resort, running after women and longing for the coming of night, that brought with it pleasure barges, colored lights and music by Verdi." Hülsenbeck had arrived in Zürich from Berlin in the winter of 1915–16 as a 23-year-old medical student to whom the war was abhorrent. He was a versatile young man with a talent for insolence, and he turned out to play a leader's role in Zürich Dada. He was poet, performer, coeditor with Hugo Ball of the Dada periodical *Cabaret Voltaire,* and a most ferocious champion of what in Switzerland passed for jazz. He fancied himself as a writer of nonsense verse ("The whole Monist Club is gathered on the steamship Meyerbeer," one passage ran, "But only the pilot has any conception of high C"), but he did not agree with another Dadaist, Tristan Tzara, that "Dada means nothing." And when he got back to Berlin in January, 1917, he saw to it that, as he said, "in Germany Dada lost its art-for-art's-sake character with its very first move."

Evenings at the Galerie Dada in Zürich were frankly eclectic: new music by Arnold Schoenberg and Alban Berg took its turn with readings from Jules Laforgue and Guillaume Apollinaire, demonstrations of "Negro dancing," and a new play by the Ex-

35. George Grosz
The Engineer Heartfield,
1920
The Museum of Modern
Art, New York

John Heartfield (1891–1968) was a master of photomontage. In this witty little portrait George Grosz used some of the techniques which Heartfield had perfected. The printed message on the cut-out section of a Berlin street (top right) reads "The best of luck in your new home"; but the new home in question is clearly a prison cell. Heartfield at that time was constantly in danger of arrest for subversive activities.

pressionist painter and playwright Oskar Kokoschka. Hülsenbeck would have none of that in Berlin. The Expressionists, in particular, seemed to him like "those famous medical quacks who promise that 'everything will soon be back to normal.'" He goes on, "Under the pretext of turning inward, the Expressionist painters and writers have banded together into a generation which already looks forward to honorable mention in the history books and a chestful of civic distinctions." The Expressionists stood for subjectivity, for the spiritual life, for the old-German Gothic world; to that extent they backed up the status quo. "Dada was not a 'made' movement," George Grosz wrote: "it was an organic product, which began as a reaction against the head-in-the-clouds attitudes of so-called high art, whose disciples brooded over cubes, and over Gothic art, while the generals were painting in blood."

DADA IN BERLIN, COLOGNE AND HANOVER

This was the state of mind in which Hülsenbeck and Raoul Hausmann wrote their Dada manifesto in Berlin in April, 1918. It called for an international revolutionary union of all creative men and women; for progressive unemployment through the mechanization of all fields of activity; for the abolition of private property; for the provision of free daily meals for creative people and intellectuals; for the remodeling of big-city life by a Dadaist advisory council; and for the regulation of all sexual activity under the supervision of a Dadaist sexual center. These proposals were put forward at what George Grosz called "the time of the turnip": a period in which it was nothing unusual for the supply of potatoes to give out and be replaced by turnips normally used as cattle fodder. The Allied blockade brought starvation daily nearer; the German Army was getting more and more demoralized; there had been the beginnings of mutiny in the German Navy as early as July, 1917; 400,000 munition workers had been on strike in Berlin. It was, if ever, a time for desperate measures; and we cannot blame the Berliners who thought of Zürich as a city not so much neutral as neutered.

Much of Berlin Dada is a matter of legend. There were bold single acts which nobody followed up, as when Johannes Baader climbed up to the pulpit in Berlin Cathedral and treated the congregation to a Dadaist harangue. There were projects well over the frontiers of fantasy, as when that same Baader planned a five-story-high "Dio-Dada-Drama" which was to encapsulate "The Greatness and the Fall of Germany." There were prosecutions for antimilitarist activity. There were publications which have clung to history as burrs cling to the jacket of a hunter. Alternative art reached its point of maximum immediacy in the Berlin of 1918–20; and though not much of it survived as museum material something of its quintessence can be seen in the photomontages which were produced by John Heartfield, George Grosz, Johannes Baader, Raoul Hausmann and Hannah Höch. Berlin is a quick-witted, skeptical city in which a certain lapidary derision stands high among conversational qualities; and in the photomontages in question that trait is carried over into art.

In any account of international Dada an invidious distinction must be made between the people who went on to be major artists of a more general sort and the people whose association with Dada is really their only claim upon us. Cologne Dada, like Berlin Dada, had its full share of glorious human oddities; but it is on Max Ernst, finally, that our attention rests. When Ernst returned to Cologne as a demobilized soldier in 1918 he sized up the situation not as a social revolutionary, like his friend Johannes Baargeld, but as an artist who had proved himself a considerable

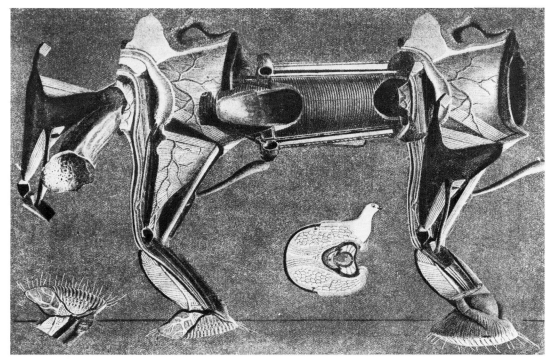

36. (*above*) Max Ernst
Untitled, 1920
Menil Family Collection, Houston, Texas

37. (*left*) Max Ernst
The Horse, He's Sick, 1920
The Museum of Modern Art, New York

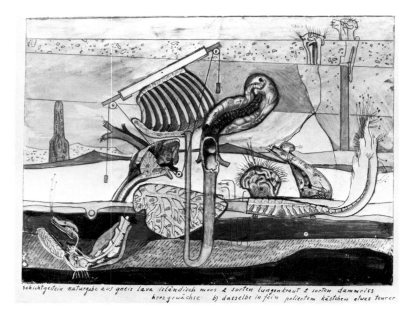

39. Max Ernst
*Stratified Rocks, Nature's Gift of Gneiss Lava Iceland Moss 2 Kinds
of Lungwort 2 Kinds of Ruptures of the Perineum Growths of the Heart (b)
The Same Thing in a Well-polished Box Somewhat More Expensive*, 1920
The Museum of Modern Art, New York

38. Max Ernst
Little Machine Constructed by Minimax Dadamax in Person, 1919
Peggy Guggenheim Foundation, Venice

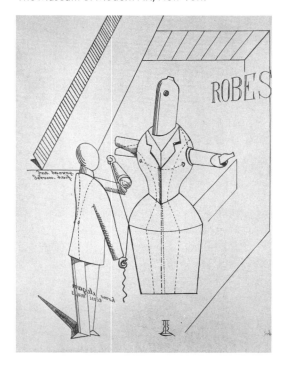

40. (*right*) Max Ernst
*Fiat Modes, Pereat Ars (Let There Be Fashion,
Down with Art)*, Plate VII: *Robes*, c. 1919
The Museum of Modern Art, New York

painter as early as 1906. He had been a member of August Macke's Young Rhineland group in Bonn before the war, he had known Jean Arp since 1914, and he had made himself familiar with the prewar art scene in Paris, Cologne and Berlin. Already as a student he had realized that the untaught scribblings of children, mad people, obsessives of all kinds might have more to contribute to modern art than anything that was taught in the academies. So it was by extension of a long-held opinion that Max Ernst spoke out in 1919 against "Everyman," who "loves Everyman's expressionists but turns away in disgust from the graffiti in public lavatories."

He was still only 28 in that year, and he had arrears of experience to make up. Until he and Baargeld went to Munich on a visit, he had no idea of the role that Arp had played in Zürich Dada; and it was from a magazine picked up by chance in a Munich bookshop that he learned what Carlo Carrà and Giorgio de Chirico had been doing in Italy. He was a convinced Dada member, who enjoyed the nickname of "Dadamax," was co-founder with Baargeld of the Rhineland branch of Dadaism (address: W/3 West Stupidia), edited its Dadaist review, *Die Schammade,* and took a leading role in the Dada exhibition which opened in Cologne in April, 1920, and was almost immediately shut down by the police. Dada owed a great deal to Max Ernst by the time he left Germany for Paris in 1921; but he owed something to Dada, too, and to the notion of a General Strike for art which Dada had been mooting since 1916. He spoke of himself in November, 1918, as "a young man who aspired to find the myth of his own time"; he had studied abnormal psychology at an early age, and he knew that what had applied to individuals before 1914 might well apply to whole societies when World War I at last came to an end. In life he was antipaternalism personified and had an especial horror of the word "duty"; if Dada could do away with the structures of obedience which had for so long been mandatory among Germans, so much the better.

Max Ernst was not so anxious to do away with art as to extend full membership to forms of statement which had previously been denied admission. This was, of course, typical of Dada; but he brought to his Dada works a steely determination, a malicious humor with overtones of intellectual terrorism, and a gift for verbal embellishment which was quite the equal of anything that had been done in that line elsewhere. At the same time he had an existence of his own outside of Dada, and interests which were independent of it. As much as Duchamp, he had that flair for irreverent conjunction which had been pioneered by Lautréamont and carried onward by Jules Laforgue, Alfred Jarry and Guillaume Apollinaire. Above all, his work was quintessentially

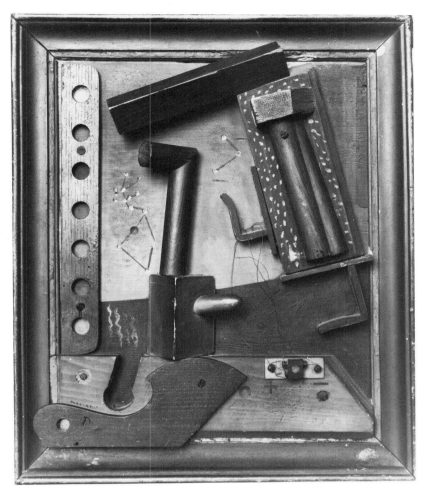

41. Max Ernst
Fruit of a Long Experience, 1919
Private collection, Geneva

modern in that he used, to still unsurpassed effect, the device of the quick cut.

The quick cut was a combination of ellipsis, on the one hand, and a well-calculated jump in the dark, on the other. Fernand Léger was quite right when he said in 1914 that modern man could be distinguished from earlier man by the fact that the number of impressions with which he had to deal was a thousand times greater. Léger himself tackled this problem both by rigorous selection and by the fragmentation or overlapping of images which would formerly have been shown complete. But only after

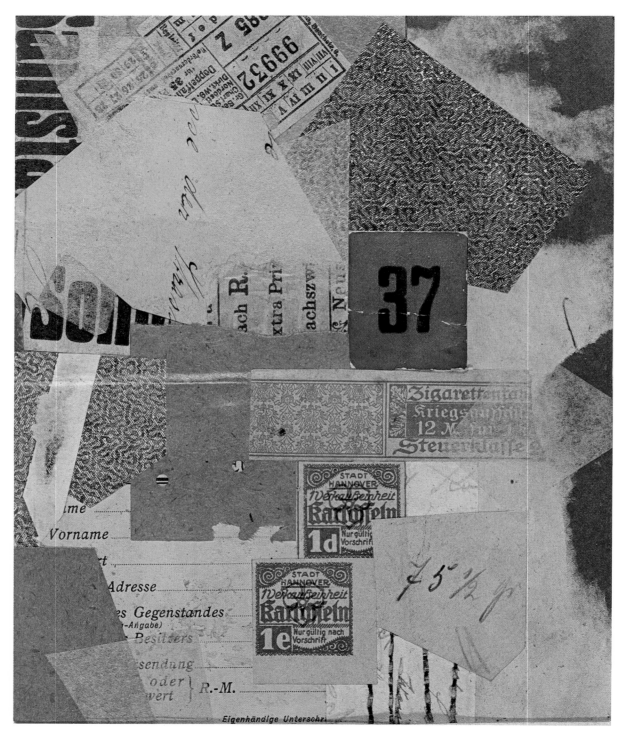

XI. Kurt Schwitters
Merz 19, 1920
Yale University Art Gallery,
New Haven, Conn.

XII. Kurt Schwitters
Merz 380: Schlotheim, 1922
Yale University Art Gallery,
New Haven, Conn.

42. Max Ernst
Here Everything Is Still Floating, 1920
The Museum of Modern Art, New York

a complete break with previous pictorial tradition could the kind of quick cutting which was perfected by Max Ernst become incorporated in the act of reading a picture. To that extent, and by making a certain nimbleness of mind mandatory among those who looked at new art, Dada created a climate in which Max Ernst could go to work.

It was in art that the quick cut and the well-calculated jump imposed themselves most vividly at this time. Anyone who looked at Max Ernst's *Here Everything is Still Floating* (fig. 42) had to adjust to an underwater scene in which a steamship came in the likeness of an anatomical drawing of a beetle seen upside down; above and to the right was a fish, seen as if in an X-ray photograph, which could also be read as a primitive airship. Air and water, soaring and swimming, anatomy and engineering—all changed places in this tiny and mysterious picture, and yet all were still present as themselves. In such pictures as these Max Ernst restructured the act of reading a work of art. He was not alone in doing it—it could be said to have begun, like so much

else, with Cubism—and the acts both of reading and of looking were, of course, being restructured in other forms of human activity also. At its most inventive, the silent cinema of the 1920s demanded of its audiences such acrobatics of attention as had never been performed before. Max Ernst knew when to tease, when to present an image directly, and when to spike the whole adventure with a long caption that darted in and out of common sense as a lizard darts in and out of the shade. What he made was not "a Dada picture" but an accelerated statement for which Dada had given the go-ahead.

Max Ernst was against Authority, as such, and it never worried him that Cologne Dada was more than once in trouble with the police. But he was not a political activist. He stood somewhat apart, therefore, from the Berlin Dadaists when they took (often from the most innocent of motives) a straight Communist line. He was his own man.

Kurt Schwitters in Hanover was his own man, too, much to the exasperation of Hülsenbeck, who called him "a highly talented petit-bourgeois." One of Schwitters' closest friends was nearer to the point when she said that he "simply didn't have a conventional bone in his body." But he did, admittedly, sit out the vicissitudes of postwar Germany in his house in Hanover, unaffected by the commitments of Dadaists elsewhere. This was the more enraging to the activists in that Schwitters was in many ways the ideal (and potentially the supreme) Dadaist. Others got up on platforms and made fools of themselves, more or less. Schwitters survives, through a gramophone recording, as one of the most extraordinary performers of the century. When he read his "Primeval Sonata"—a long poem made up entirely of wordless sounds—it was as if there had come into existence a completely new mode of human expression, by turns hilarious and terrifying, elemental and precisely engineered. Others dreamed of reconciling art and language, music and speech, the living room and the cathedral, the stage and the unspoiled forest. Schwitters had the sweep of mind not only to dream of these things but to carry them out, within the physical limits available to him. All this he did in the name of an invented concept which he called "Merz."

Merz (derived from the second syllable of the German word *Kommerz*) was a working name which Schwitters used to identify all his activities (and himself, also, at times: one of his publications was signed Kurt Merz Schwitters). "Everything had broken down," Schwitters wrote of the beginnings of Merz, "and new things had to be made out of fragments. It was like an image of the revolution within me—not as it was, but as it might have been." Schwitters was a one-man encyclopedia of Dada preoccupations. He was painter, collagist, sculptor, poet, performer,

43. Kurt Schwitters
Drawing A 2: Hansi-Schokolade, 1918
The Museum of Modern Art, New York

44. Kurt Schwitters
Merz 83: Drawing F, 1920
The Museum of Modern Art, New York

typographer, visionary architect. He was the consummation of Dada. He, as much as anyone, completed the union of art and non-art which had always been fundamental to Dada. In intention he was one of our century's great reconcilers: as a roller-back of boundaries he has still to be surpassed. It was never easy, and it is now impossible, to see his achievement in its totality. That achievement was summed up in the union of the arts which he effected in his own houses, first in Hanover, later in Norway, and finally, on a much-diminished scale, in England. What he did in each case was to remake the language of living. The house was

taken over, room by room and later upward through the ceiling. It was reshaped in various radical ways and filled slowly and consistently with material objects which were neither architecture, nor painting, nor sculpture, nor reading matter, but an as-yet-unnamed amalgam and crossbreeding of all four of them. Like Duchamp's *Large Glass,* the first Merz building (in Hanover) had an elaborate program which was conceived and added to in a spirit of irony; but whereas the *Large Glass* is Voltairean in its mockery and its power to disconcert, Schwitters was by nature a healer, and the lesson of his work is that men are free to remake

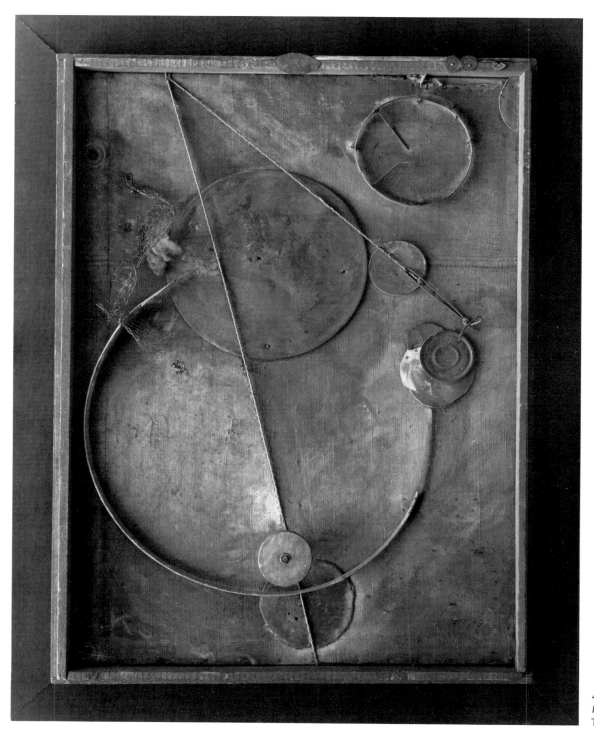

45. Kurt Schwitters
Revolving, 1919
The Museum of Modern Art, New York

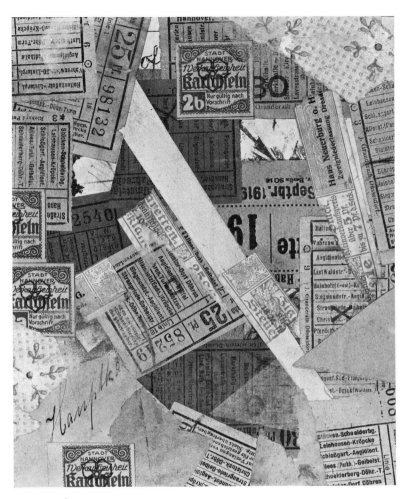

46. Kurt Schwitters
Merz 22, 1920
The Museum of Modern Art, New York

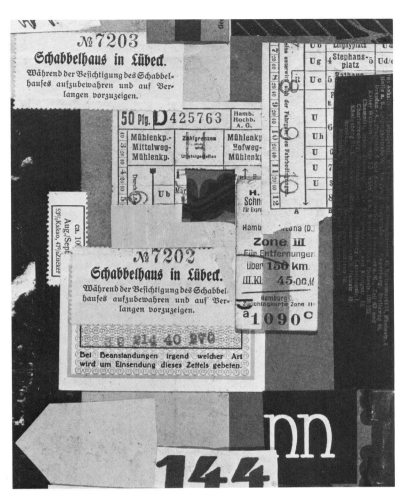

47. Kurt Schwitters
Merz 458, c. 1920–22
The Museum of Modern Art, New York

the world from its beginnings. This applies to individual elements within the world—the theater, for instance: every experimental theater owes something to Schwitters—and it applies to our environment in its totality.

Most people know Schwitters by what he called his Merz paintings and Merz drawings. These too can be read as an effort of reconciliation, insofar as they often draw upon the achievement of others, notably on the constructed objects produced by

Picasso and, more generally, on Synthetic Cubism, with its overlapping flat planes and its mainly rectilinear structure. Sometimes they stand for the anti-aesthetic attitudes of Dada—as, for instance, in *Revolving* (fig. 45), where the materials used are as brutish as they could be. Yet the effect of *Revolving* is to create from those materials a reminder that our much-battered world is part of a planetary system which goes on revolving no matter how grievously we misgovern ourselves. Sometimes, equally,

48. Kurt Schwitters
Merz 379: Potsdamer, 1922
The Museum of Modern Art, New York

they elaborate ideas explored elsewhere by Dada: the strange power which resides in printed matter that has been removed from its original context, for instance. And sometimes they draw on other forms of art: on the color theories of Robert Delaunay, or the affinities with nature of Franz Marc, or the collapsing cosmos of Kandinsky. But Schwitters was not "a borrower," in any disparaging sense. His borrowings were metamorphosed by a poetry that was entirely his own.

Nor did he have the apocalyptic ambitions that Dada had sometimes claimed for itself. He was for an alternative art; and he produced it, as well as anyone. But he knew that an alternative is not necessarily a substitute. "I never meant," he wrote in 1926, "to demonstrate that henceforward pictures could only be made out of junk. I believe that if my paintings are at all successful I have somewhat enlarged the domains of art, without thereby endangering the standing of great works of art in any age." Remarks of this kind reveal the angelic modesty which so vexed the big talkers of full-time Dada; and as most of Schwitters' collages will go comfortably into an overcoat pocket, there is a risk of their being discounted as charm-school work of only marginal importance. Delicious they are, but their small size should not deceive us. It is only very rarely that we find in art a body of work that so tenaciously persuades us to look more closely, and to look in a new way. The lessons of this particular alternative art are still being digested.

Dada as a collective adventure did not take over the world, as had been hoped for by some of its more extravagant supporters. And by 1922 it had evolved—in Paris, above all—into a primarily literary movement that was marked over and over again by spectacular clashes of temperament. But it is to the credit of Dada that it acted as the lever on which whole new departments of modernity swung into view. Perhaps Richard Hülsenbeck spoke truer than he knew when he said in 1919 that "Dada is the only savings bank that pays interest in eternity."

SUGGESTED READINGS

General

Baigell, Matthew. *History of American Painting*. (World of Art ser.)
New York, Praeger, 1971.

Brown, Milton W. *American Painting from The Armory Show to the Depression*.
Princeton, N.J., Princeton University Press, 1955.

Dunlop, Ian. *The Shock of the New*.
New York, American Heritage Press, 1972.

Philadelphia Museum of Art. *Louise and Walter Arensberg Collection*, 1954.
Introduction by Henry Clifford.

Rose, Barbara. *American Art Since 1900: A Critical History*. (World of Art ser.)
New York, Praeger, 1967.

Dadaism

Barr, Alfred H., Jr. *Fantastic Art, Dada, and Surrealism*. Reprint. First publ. 1937.
New York, Arno for The Museum of Modern Art, 1970.

Bigsby, C. W. *Dada and Surrealism*. (The Critical Idiom ser.)
London, Methuen, 1972.

Coutts-Smith, Kenneth. *Dada*.
London, Studio Vista; New York, E. P. Dutton, 1970.

Hülsenbeck, Richard, ed. *Dada Almanach*.
Millerton, N.Y., Something Else Press, 1966.

Lippard, Lucy R., ed. *Dadas on Art*.
Englewood Cliffs, N.J., Prentice-Hall, 1971.

Motherwell, Robert, ed. *Dada Painters and Poets*.
New York, Wittenborn, 1951.

Richter, Hans. *Dada: Art and Anti-Art*.
New York, McGraw-Hill, 1965.

Rubin, William S. *Dada, Surrealism and Their Heritage*.
New York, The Museum of Modern Art, 1968.

Rubin, William S. *Dada and Surrealist Art*.
New York, Abrams, 1969.

Marcel Duchamp

Duchamp, Marcel. *Notes and Projects for the Large Glass*.
New York, Abrams, 1969.

Hopps, Walter; Linde, Ulf, and Schwarz, Arturo. *Marcel Duchamp: Readymades, etc., 1913–1964*. (Texts in Italian, French and English.)
Paris, Le Terrain Vague, 1964.

Schwarz, Arturo. *The Complete Works of Marcel Duchamp*.
New York, Abrams. 1969.

Tomkins, Calvin. *The World of Marcel Duchamp*. (Time-Life Library of Art ser.)
New York, Time-Life, 1966.

Tomkins, Calvin. *Bride and the Bachelors: The Heretical Courtship in Modern Art*. Rev. ed.
New York, Viking, 1968.

Raymond Duchamp-Villon

Hamilton, George H. *Raymond Duchamp-Villon, 1876–1918*.
New York, Walker, 1967.

Max Ernst

Alexandrian, Sarane. *Max Ernst*.
Los Angeles, O'Hara, 1972.

Di San Lazzaro, G., ed. *Homage to Max Ernst*.
New York, Tudor, 1972.

Ernst, Max. *Beyond Painting and other Writings by the Artist and His Friends*. (Documents of Modern Art ser.)
New York, Wittenborn, 1948.

Lieberman, William S. *Max Ernst*. Reprint. First publ. 1961.
New York, Arno for The Museum of Modern Art, 1972.

Russell, John. *Max Ernst: Life and Work*.
New York, Abrams, 1967.

Schneede, Uwe M. *The Essential Max Ernst*.
London, Thames and Hudson, 1972.

Spies, Werner. *The Return of La Belle Jardinière. Max Ernst, 1950–1970*.
New York, Abrams, 1971.

Fernand Léger

Delevoy, Robert L. *Léger: Biographical and Critical Study*.
Geneva, Skira, 1962.

Francia, Peter de. *Léger's "The Great Parade."*
London, Cassell, 1969.

Kurt Schwitters

Schmalenbach, Werner. *Kurt Schwitters*.
New York, Abrams, 1967.

Steinitz, Kate Trauman. *Kurt Schwitters: A Portrait from Life*.
Berkeley, University of California Press, 1968.

Themerson, Stefan. *Kurt Schwitters in England*.
London, Gaberbocchus Press, 1958.

Dimensions: height precedes width; another dimension, depth, is given for sculptures and constructions where relevant. Foreign titles are in English, except in cases where the title does not translate or is better known in its original form. Asterisked titles indicate works reproduced in color.

Arp, Jean (Hans)
(1887–1966)

Madame Torso with a Wavy Hat, 1916 (fig. 33)
Wood relief, 16 x 10 inches
Kunstmuseum, Bern

Forest, 1916 (pl. IX)
Painted wood, 12½ x 8¼ inches
Penrose Collection, London

Squares Arranged According to the Laws of Chance, 1917 (fig. 34)
Collage of cut and pasted papers, gouache, ink and bronze paint, 13⅛ x 10¼ inches
The Museum of Modern Art, New York
Gift of Philip Johnson

Bruce, Patrick Henry
(1880–1937)

Composition II, c. 1916–17 (fig. 2)
Oil on canvas, 38¼ x 51 inches
Yale University Art Gallery, New Haven, Conn.
Gift of Collection Société Anonyme

Courbet, Gustave
(1819–1877)

The Robing of the Bride, 1865–70 (fig. 25)
Oil on canvas, 74 x 99 inches
Smith College Museum of Art, Northampton, Mass.

Covert, John R.
(b. 1882)

Time, 1919 (fig. 8)
Oil and upholstery tacks on composition board, 25⅝ x 23½ inches
Yale University Art Gallery, New Haven, Conn.
Gift of Collection Société Anonyme

Davis, Stuart
(1894–1964)

Lucky Strike, 1921 (fig. 14)
Oil on canvas, 33¼ x 18 inches
The Museum of Modern Art, New York
Gift of the American Tobacco Company Inc.

Itlksez, 1921 (fig. 15)
Watercolor and collage on paper, 22 x 16 inches
Lane Foundation, Leominster, Mass.

Dove, Arthur G.
(1880–1946)

Nature Symbolized, No. 2, 1911 (fig. 5)
Pastel, 17⅞ x 21½ inches
The Art Institute of Chicago
The Alfred Stieglitz Collection

Portrait of Alfred Stieglitz, 1925 (fig. 10)
Assemblage: camera lens, photographic plate, clock and watch springs, steel wool on cardboard, 15⅞ x 12⅛ inches
The Museum of Modern Art, New York
Purchase

The Intellectual, 1925 (fig. 16)
Assemblage: magnifying glass, bone, moss, bark and a scale glued or nailed on varnished cloth, mounted on wood panel, 17 x 7⅛ inches
The Museum of Modern Art, New York
The Philip L. Goodwin Collection

Duchamp, Marcel
(1887–1968)

The Bride, 1912 (fig. 24)
Oil on canvas, 35⅛ x 21¾ inches
Philadelphia Museum of Art
The Louise and Walter Arensberg Collection

The Passage from the Virgin to the Bride, 1912 (pl. VI)
Oil on canvas, 23⅜ x 21¼ inches
The Museum of Modern Art, New York
Purchase

Bicycle Wheel, (1951, third version after lost original of 1913) (fig. 23)
Readymade: bicycle wheel mounted on painted wooden stool, 50½ x 25½ x 16⅝ inches
The Museum of Modern Art, New York
The Sidney and Harriet Janis Collection

Chocolate Grinder, No. 1, 1913 (fig. 19)
Oil on canvas, 24⅜ x 25½ inches
Philadelphia Museum of Art
The Louise and Walter Arensberg Collection

Chocolate Grinder, No. 2, 1914 (fig. 18)
Oil, thread and pencil on canvas, 25½ x 21¼ inches
Philadelphia Museum of Art
The Louise and Walter Arensberg Collection

Three Standard Stoppages, 1913–14 (fig. 31)
Three threads glued upon three glass panels, each: 49⅜ x 7¼ inches; plus three flat wooden strips repeating the curves of the threads
The Museum of Modern Art, New York
Katherine S. Dreier Bequest

Network of Stoppages, 1914 (fig. 32)
Oil on canvas, 58¼ x 77⅝ inches
The Museum of Modern Art, New York
Abby Aldrich Rockefeller Fund and gift of Mrs. William Sisler

The Bride Stripped Bare by her Bachelors, Even (Large Glass), 1915–23 (pl. VII)
Oil, lead wire and foil, dust and varnish on glass (in two parts), 9 feet 1¼ inches x 5 feet 9⅛ inches
Philadelphia Museum of Art
Bequest of Katherine S. Dreier

With Hidden Noise, 1916 (fig. 26)
Ball of twine, two brass plates and four long bolts, "assisted" by the artist, 5 x 5 x 5 inches
Philadelphia Museum of Art
The Louise and Walter Arensberg Collection

Apolinère Enameled (Girl with Bedstead), 1916–17 (pl. VIII)
Painted tin advertisement for Sapolin Enamel, altered and added to by the artist, 9¼ x 13¼ inches
Philadelphia Museum of Art
The Louise and Walter Arensberg Collection

To Be Looked at with One Eye, Close to, for Almost an Hour, 1918 (fig. 27)
Framed double glass panel with lead, oil, rusted metal, magnifying glass and "silver scratching" on glass (broken), 20⅛ x 16⅛ x 1⅜ inches
The Museum of Modern Art, New York
Katherine S. Dreier Bequest

Fresh Widow, 1920 (fig. 28)
Miniature French window: painted wood frame
    with 8 panes of glass, covered with waxed
    leather, 30½ x 17⅝ inches
The Museum of Modern Art, New York
Katherine S. Dreier Bequest

Why Not Sneeze, Rose Sélavy? (1964 replica of
    original of 1921) (fig. 30)
Assisted readymade: marble blocks (in the shape
    of lumps of sugar), thermometer, wood and
    cuttlefish bone in a small bird cage,
    4⅞ x 8¾ x 6⅜ inches
The Museum of Modern Art, New York
Gift of Galleria Schwarz

The Large Glass Completed, 1965–66 (fig. 29)
Colored engraving on pearl-finished porcelain
    (3rd impression), 20 x 13 inches
Galleria Schwarz Collection, Milan

Ernst, Max
(b. 1891)

*Little Machine Constructed by Minimax Dadamax
    in Person,* 1919 (fig. 38)
Pencil, watercolor and gouache on paper,
    18 x 12⅛ inches
Peggy Guggenheim Foundation, Venice

Fruit of a Long Experience, 1919 (fig. 41)
Painted wood and metal, 18 x 15 inches
Private collection, Geneva

*Fiat Modes, Pereat Ars (Let There Be Fashion,
    Down with Art),* Plate VII: *Robes,* c. 1919
    (fig. 40)
Set of eight lithographs, 17⅛ x 12 inches
The Museum of Modern Art, New York
Purchase

Here Everything Is Still Floating, 1920 (fig. 42)
Pasted photo engravings, 4⅛ x 4⅞ inches
The Museum of Modern Art, New York
Purchase

Untitled, 1920 (fig. 36)
Collage, 2⅝ x 5⅝ inches
Menil Family Collection, Houston, Texas

*Stratified Rocks, Nature's Gift of Gneiss Lava
    Iceland Moss 2 Kinds of Lungwort 2 Kinds of
    Ruptures of the Perineum Growths of the
    Heart (b) The Same Thing in a Well-polished
    Box Somewhat More Expensive,* 1920 (fig. 39)
Anatomical engraving altered with gouache and
    pencil, 6 x 8⅛ inches
The Museum of Modern Art, New York
Purchase

The Horse, He's Sick, 1920 (fig. 37)
Pasted papers, pencil and ink, 5¾ x 8½ inches
The Museum of Modern Art, New York
Purchase

Grosz, George
(1893–1959)

The Engineer Heartfield, 1920 (fig. 35)
Watercolor and collage, 16½ x 12 inches
The Museum of Modern Art, New York
Gift of A. Conger Goodyear

Hartley, Marsden
(1877–1943)

Portrait of a German Officer, 1914 (fig. 7)
Oil on canvas, 68¼ x 41⅜ inches
The Metropolitan Museum of Art, New York
The Alfred Stieglitz Collection, 1949

Léger, Fernand
(1881–1955)

The Card Players, 1917 (fig. 1)
Oil on canvas, 50⅞ x 76 inches
Rijksmuseum Kröller-Müller, Otterlo, Holland

MacDonald-Wright, Stanton
(b. 1890)

Abstraction on Spectrum (Organization 5), 1914
    (pl. III)
Oil on canvas, 30 x 24 inches
Des Moines Art Center, Des Moines, Iowa
Nathan Emory Coffin Memorial Collection

Man Ray
(b. 1890)

A.D. MCMXIV, 1914 (fig. 3)
Oil, 37 x 69½ inches
Philadelphia Museum of Art
The A. E. Gallatin Collection

Interior, 1915 (fig. 13)
Watercolor and silver paper, 23¾ x 17¼ inches
Philadelphia Museum of Art
The A. E. Gallatin Collection

* *The Rope Dancer Accompanies Herself with Her
    Shadows,* 1916 (pl. II)
Oil on canvas, 52 x 73⅜ inches
The Museum of Modern Art, New York
Gift of G. David Thompson

Rrose Sélavy (Portrait of Marcel Duchamp), 1923
    (fig. 22)
Oil on canvas, 23½ x 19½ inches
Private collection, New York

Matisse, Henri
(1869–1954)

* *Bathers by a River,* 1916–17 (pl. I)
Oil on canvas, 8 feet 7 inches x 12 feet 10 inches
The Art Institute of Chicago
Worcester Collection

O'Keeffe, Georgia
(b. 1887)

Evening Star III, 1917 (fig. 6)
Watercolor, 9 x 11⅞ inches
The Museum of Modern Art, New York
Mr. and Mrs. Donald B. Straus Fund

Picabia, Francis
(1879–1953)

* *I See Again in Memory my Dear Udnie,* 1914
    (pl. IV)
Oil on canvas, 98½ x 78¼ inches
The Museum of Modern Art, New York
Hillman Periodicals Fund

Here, This Is Stieglitz, 1915 (fig. 11)
Ink, 29⅞ x 20 inches
The Metropolitan Museum of Art, New York
The Alfred Stieglitz Collection, 1949

* *Very Rare Picture Upon the Earth,* 1915 (pl. V)
Gilt and silver paint and collage of wooden forms
    on cardboard, 44¾ x 34 inches
Peggy Guggenheim Foundation, Venice

The Blessed Virgin, 1920 (fig. 21)
Reproduced in *391,* Paris, No. 12, March, 1920

Amorous Parade, 1917 (fig. 12)
Oil on canvas, 38 x 29 inches
Mr. and Mrs. Morton G. Neumann, Chicago

The Child Carburetor, c. 1919 (fig. 20)
Oil, gilt, pencil and metallic paint on plywood,
    49¾ x 39⅞ inches
The Solomon R. Guggenheim Museum, New York

* *Plumes,* c. 1923–27? (pl. X)
Ripolin, feathers, macaroni, cane and corn plasters
    on canvas in a dowelled frame, 46⅞ x 30⅞
    inches
Galleria Schwarz Collection, Milan

Schamberg, Morton
(1881–1918)

God, c. 1918 (fig. 9)
Miter box and plumbing trap, 10½ inches high
Philadelphia Museum of Art
The Louise and Walter Arensberg Collection

Schwitters, Kurt
(1887–1948)

Drawing A 2: Hansi-Schokolade, 1918 (fig. 43)
Collage of colored papers and wrappers,
    7⅛ x 5¾ inches
The Museum of Modern Art, New York
Purchase

Revolving, 1919 (fig. 45)
Collage of wood, metal and cardboard, wool,
    wire, leather and oil on canvas, 48⅜ x 35
    inches (sight)
The Museum of Modern Art, New York
Advisory Committee Fund

* *Merz 19,* 1920 (pl. XI)
Collage, 7¼ x 5⅞ inches
Yale University Art Gallery, New Haven, Conn.
Gift of Collection Société Anonyme

Merz 83: Drawing F, 1920 (fig. 44)
Collage of cut paper wrappers, announcements
    and tickets, 5¾ x 4½ inches
The Museum of Modern Art, New York
Katherine S. Dreier Bequest

Merz 22, 1920 (fig. 46)
Collage of railroad and bus tickets, wallpaper and
    ration stamps, 6⅝ x 5⅜ inches
The Museum of Modern Art, New York
Katherine S. Dreier Bequest

Merz 458, c. 1920–22 (fig. 47)
Collage of streetcar tickets, wrappers, ration
    stamps and colored paper, 7 x 5⅝ inches
The Museum of Modern Art, New York
Katherine S. Dreier Bequest

* *Merz 380: Schlotheim,* 1922 (pl. XII)
Collage, 7½ x 5¼ inches
Yale University Art Gallery, New Haven, Conn.
Gift of Collection Société Anonyme

Merz 379: Potsdamer, 1922 (fig. 48)
Collage of papers and cloth, 7⅛ x 5¾ inches
The Museum of Modern Art, New York
Purchase

Villon, Jacques
(1875–1963)

Marcel Duchamp, 1953 (fig. 17)
Etching, 12⅝ x 9⅝ inches
The Museum of Modern Art, New York
Gift of Louis Carré

Weber, Max
(1881–1961)

Chinese Restaurant, 1915 (fig. 4)
Oil on canvas, 40 x 48 inches
Whitney Museum of American Art, New York